WHEN THE PRISM BREAKS

A POETRY COLLECTION

GARIMA SINGH

Dedication

Dedicated to the moments that haunt but eventually evolve us into a version we never believed was buried deep within our hearts

Preface

We often try to escape some memories that keep us tied up to the bottom. Telling ourselves that we have passed that phase or moment and are truly moving out of that chapter of life is a different thing. But all those pile-up emotions eventually come out of our consciousness through one thing: acceptance. This disperses our feelings into many lights; we just have to go through some new experiences. This poetry collection is about those spontaneous feelings that reflect the different emotions and filter our own selves, which evolve out of the isolation we leave to befriend ourselves first.

Acknowledgements

Sincerely, thanks to my family and friends and the people who have come into my life.

1. Train at the Junction

It leaves,
no matter how dense the fog is
how old the tracks are,
the train departs at the right second
it is never too late
even if the watch keeps swaying for a few more courses
the moment it leaves is the time,
unbiased and cruel
sometimes fair.
But it leaves
it does not shed tears or stay quiet,
no mercy to the either sides,
it runs at its own speed.
The junction welcomes it warmly
to bid farewell to the departed
the white coaches do not spare a minute,
and it fades away from the junction
just as planned.

2. The Night

It's better not to see the alleys
better to avoid the thick wires
crawling silently in the dark tone
as the beautiful moon fades.
What more can I capture
nothing, on the brink now.
It's better to lie down,
better to turn away
anyway, the windows block the wind
cold blunt wind
what else can I behold
months and months go to waste.
It's better to leave the sleepy city
better under the white sheets
music of the yellow whispers
one more play of the puppets
cites another night
into the boxes of marbles.
So it's better to rise somewhere away
Better to see the Reds and greens

3. Prize

Unhappiness comes with a prize
big and wild
green road of vague dreams
with flowers falling from million skies
all set and all done
if only one is ready, how colourful it would be
and how beautiful it would float
unhappiness comes with the rain
cold and blue.

4. Warmly, to Home

Now you tell me, how do I put you in my verses,
because verses come out of grief
and you lie in my happy memories,
how can I put you in my grey diary
how can I make this crossover happen
I can pick a pen if you insist,
but I stop thinking
how would I wet the pages to glow in the darkness
how can I answer the devils in my head
and how can I build a bridge for you to walk to this
ghastly mansion?
Tell me, how can my words carry your smiles and
summers
Because verses only walk when it is raining.

5. Vintage Edition

So yes, somebody had it too
right here in this huge library
she succeeded in finding it in the crowd of countless
suitors
squeezed up among the tight bindings
waiting to be issued to spill out more secrets
to be coloured with newly filled Inks and raw pencils
like a candlelight,
possibility, she might pull up some new secret
or a new world
maybe hanging out in the gardens or on the couch
but surely it would be intense.
Those old leaves are more attractive and fragile
half yellow, half brown, perhaps half read too
yet, aesthetic like a palace old
at the back, a list of past outings
with previous lovers
few are too old,
she remembers the inks very well of course.
How could one forget a past lover?
Some in blue, some in black, some are blurred
the new might not see it, but
she clearly remembers the moments they were smeared
on her plates,

how it turned more beautiful with every sway
how she flew her pages as if dancing on a stage.
Bless the dance partner
this one would not get rid of her enchantment
so easily
How could she? After all, she is vintage; she is rare.

6. Grey Happiness

As the first sight goes on the
beautiful writing on the yellow chart paper
I recall the jovial faces
of December gone,
sisters and jewelleries of shiny nights,
sparkling garden of crowded smiles
and the wet happiness of unwearied eyes,
so much left in the white box of bricks
while the sound of the pause dances
invisible in the living room.
And they say it's the biggest dream for the family
God's grace on the rest of us.
Happiness it is, indeed
of satisfaction, of blessings.
As the first sight goes on the
grey happiness, I recall the jovial faces
of December long.

7. Highest Point

Everybody is right, and nobody denies
the primary ritual of the world,
flows down with every generation until
it finds the highest point,
but it took me to Heidegger, fallenness
and its discovery.
I wish to escape, and I wish to follow
I pinch my arms to wake myself up from a long siesta,
and all I feel is pain; I am not asleep,
happy they are, once in a lifetime, it is
but the price comes with the prize
red and green
Here I am on the old pedestal,
the prize unburdens the strains
dry and raw.

8. Old Calender

That is how it all ends,
in turmoil and chaos
filled my room with the empty chairs,
moving here and there
by the silent cold wind.
The leaves do not fly anymore
or perhaps they too are untouched,
time is a healer, as they quote,
but can not pass this reverie
I see it as the only constant that moves
only in the wall clocks.
All are drowned; not one is alone,
Knocking is gone and the slippers stay new
hanging cane and tidy hall
It will be the same tomorrow
with a different calendar, the new date.
But calendars do not heal
nothing can heal,
It has gone; it has also gone.

9. 7:45 pm

So much happens in that one minute
when the bags are lifted on the carrier,
leaving back the frozen spaces
leftovers of the empty rose perfume
and a second after the fading jokes,
on the plain bedsheets.
So much happens one minute later
when all is left is the photo album
stretching both the curves
lit up eyes in the dark
to wait for one more minute
and then close the gates with one less inside.

10. One or Two, More or Less

A hundred times, one or two, more or less
Under the dark, moony shadow on the round table
Sometimes in the tea shop with half a cup of first sight
And right in the middle of the dense trees
beside the red buildings
Just similar to the market area
where I stumbled into the narrow alley
Which took me back to the post office,
where he asked for a pen and some glue
And I helped him how to tape an envelope
And sometimes the birthday spots under the midnight
moon
Clapping with a tilted head
Nights are frequent, especially at the bus stop,
where he stood silently just to be there
And most of the time, around the mountains
 and beside the river of dreams
Which wraps us in the little hut of my head
Married and happy, cheerful and complete
That's how all the first meetings wake me
In my head,
Writes my nights and days of reds and greens
That's how I forget how many times we introduced

ourselves

Yes I have met a hundred times, one or two, more or less

11. The Women in Fire

13

She was the mother and the nurturer,
she was the consort of the recreator
she had shackles in the divine palms,
whose beholder brought her
to the land of the dead.
So she chose to purge the defiled birth,
the fire inside the mortal flesh burned
every nail of the pale hands,
engulfed the whole universe,
The black body of ashes
lying near the kund
flying to the Great Lake, to the third eye,
until the snow cooed it again.

She was a wife, and she was Earth herself
she was the queen of the Gods,
she walked on fire, surrounded by a million bows.
She indeed remembered the eyes that choked her heart,
and the purifier's bow to the purity itself.
But what could injure the numinous soul,
when the Sudarshan is beside her
her people, blind and cruel,
when the moaning fire stood cool
blisters of suffering in her soul.

So the mortal turned to the Mother Earth
To the great sea, to the third world,
Until the lord came back again.

When one ended her life,
and the other walked through it,
she was born out of the fire
she was the oath and the sword,
death worshipped her, wind bowed to her,
the rain amused her, and the herbs adorned her,
when the tears of humiliation soaked the grand hall
she cleansed it with her long locks of blood.
The land of the gods witnessed the wrath
and the dark lady in the middle,
she let her hair burn in rage,
until the world tied it again.

12. The Sign

15

What would you call it when you see it

invisible, yet in colours

no touch, no crash

a knock

a step hangs as a warning, and sometimes

a riding

what would you call it

soaring like an old myth, waiting in time's greatest game

a room devoid of sound

windows open

silent chimes

and the blip of the postman's letter

you hear it, and you invert back at

that blip

what would you call it when you know the colour

the touch

the address

the sign.

13. April

In the dark days of the sunrise,
I saw the covered faces
frowned eyebrows with green hope,
In the gloomy street of the evening
I saw the masked boy
grabbing the falling kite,
a stone tied on a long thread
In the cold balcony of the sunset,
I saw the crowded nest
yellow grains and the happy faces.

14. The Fallen Arrow

A life it was, miserable and bruised throughout,
Bundled in a golden cloth floating in the river,
There in a veil, crying, hiding her face in pain,
Her long, expensive silk flowed freely
And the pierced heart by her own arrow.

The river was crying, holding the little boy,
Warm were the wind,
The yellow silk was not wet yet
As if the river rowed it in its own tears
Streaming towards the shore, the lavish basket
Carrying the load of not just gold
To the ones who needed to heal the wounded arrow

Birth of dreams and zeal shone in his eyes
To become the fiercest archer in the world
Amid all the humiliation and suffering
Empty-handed he was, but measured the long walk
To the great hill, to the great ones
God, he submitted all of his wooden arrows

Rivers and sky trained the God's son
Poured courage and kindness into the man,
So naturally, he stands in the crowd

But they saw only the golden armour and the vibrant
ears
It surely was his deepest wound, bled by the invisible
arrow.

Pity to him, the crown was lustrous than him
pink soft clothes, braided him well
However, the body they saw was
Wretched and ghastly
One in the thousands, he looked straight at the sun
As he could be healed by only the yellow arrow

One must be a demigod to overcome the wrath
But only a human drowns in a river of doom
pain he beheld that he let loose his fiery tongue
All the fame just vanished like the red tint
Revenge won; he lost, as he shot the fire with his filthy
arrow

War he dreamt in all of his sleep
God's favourites were now on the front
My brothers, my pain, my purpose
Screaming into his whole identity at the end
The salt, after all, was much cleaner than his blood
As he bent the rusted arrow

Death and weeping were all in vain

Standing in the field brought the cage
He was dreading to open up
One last chance could transform all
The name, the blood, the fame
All lost, and all won, life now lifeless on the final arrow.

15. Time's Greatest Plot

You change everything, you will change everything,
you, the most loyal of them
remain the same
never show your apparel, you claim to unveil all of us.
What wheels do you have that never stop?
never puncture,
sometimes you call
sometimes, you whisper in my ears to run slower.
You, the immortal of all,
put your rule over us, but
never change your words
sometimes, I see your sly smile and
sometimes, I feel your balm
I know you linger over all my woes, even my wound
you serve me both unease and patience
I know you will never change, but you will change
and I, looking back, would be stunned
to say, "O my God! What have you done to me?".

16. Window Seat

Not everyone gets the window seat,
lurking between the three grills and watches the reapers
who fly with the birds
and dance with the peacocks,
who drowns in a half-sunk house, and the
intense clouds, ready to shower,
who waits for the wooden basket on Mama's back
who smile at the barefoot children's laughter and
the sweaty shirts,
eventually reach a new life.

There are some in the middle,
their baggage under the seats
and phones in the pocket
hanging head on both sides
drooling and trespassing on the other land
passes the monotony
wake up when the journey stops
and forget all.

Another few
peeping outside and
searching for one breath of fresh air
smothered, far from the window

who hear the sound of the engines
and sway with the tree's rhythm
asking the window seat
which one of the two is the better bowler?
Not everyone remembers the windowpane
but some do,
not everyone captures the journey,
some do.

17. When the Prism Breaks

Paperweight and diamonds
you change with the seasons,
a closer sight, a dash of fissure
yet you roll around, a playful girl.
As if the poles of fate are transcending
the only chance of breathing.
Why to rush
when you know to polish your faces
Rusting would indeed be horrific,
than crashing apart on the floor
Colourless, is it?
Why to soak yourself in rains of hope then?
carrying your rainbow is all your power.
A beam of light and hope,
and you see the blush all around
a stream of love and care
and you leave your colours down
It is you who knows all of you,
all of the summers, all of the winters
all the blues and yellows
only to let it through you
is not so difficult but gracious
you own the edges; you hold the corners

only to let the lights disperse,
Is not a chance, but a victory.

18. The Groom

It can never be what it should be,
weeks and months shifted in the calendar
but the stories are still warm
tragic, coarse, sour, horrible,
and a few more dysphemism
suited well to the residue of the past.
Now, the pictures would speak
the frame would sparkle
but my dress is the same.
She is on my left
just like her
in reds and goldens
beautiful and bride
yet my picture looks the same
glimpse of a rotten smile,
seems easy for everybody, perhaps
they come for the feast.
I see the new faces pasted on the old stage
the rituals I did the first time
was meaningful for sure.
What about now?
Would I do it again?
just smile; I did it earlier
the cameras know how to lie

flashes make it effortless

because I do not trust myself; it pains my face

it was not the first time

I can't be the one anymore,

and if I can't be the one now,

then it can never be what it should be.

19. January Rains

January rains
an uninvited guest,
grass is cold already
welcoming it again,
nobody comes out to touch it,
nobody is aware
closed windows, wet and moist
but no fragrance of mud cheer,
because the rain is strange
and the clouds are, too,
but the time is gone
all that is left is tired dew.
If we wait, will it come back?
lustrous and green,
to fill this screaming crack
just the way it had been.
January rains
like the pole sunrise,
faded past in the sky
come back alive.

20. The Fruit Basket

Does it also feel the muffling
of the brown closed packet
and the huddled oranges with
two apples
gossiping about the air of the neighbours?
Or does the halved ginger really
try to sneak inside the culmination ceremony
of the owners
icing the plates they once shared?
Is it proper to rot together
crammed and faded
to avoid the gathering party?
Or should the course of time
decide the shelf space they must
keep to restart the laughter?
It takes a hundred plunges into the
fog of thoughts
to restock the table,
until you are ready to
sprinkle the salt on the sliced
pineapple, which flawlessly fills
the corner of the basket.
After all, they come in various shapes,
they all know where to slide

and embrace the apple peel
you put inside the crate a second ago
and once you dare to design the platter again,
you know where the
crumpled packet must be tucked.
It seems colourful and fresh
rather than rolling out from the holes,
it stays higher and luscious
rather than stagnant along with the
dingy corners of the fruit basket.

21. Murals

Just a few fading murals remain now,
who talks, not laying a sight on me
Day, night, noon, unaware of the time.
Suddenly, unveil a forgotten scene to me
a sort of friendship, they have bonded now
as they melt the mellow tune in me.
And when I walk all on my own,
they chatter to the leaves and gossip to the pebbles for
me
Well, it has been years with them, I know
yet in a certain unease, they wrap me.
Indeed, they carry some of my ghostly secrets
might be the reason they pity me,
In my sack of dust, they hide their gentle smile
and still reside without remorse with me.
The few fading murals remain now,
talks, not laying a sight on me

22. Beside the Peak

I wonder what the mountaineer sensed,
when she carried the kit
inside her large bag to begin,
the journey to the top.
trainings and lessons in survival
was crucial, or
mustering all her courage to take the step
was the utmost.
There might be the pressure,
be it atmospheric or the creepings in the mind
pushing her upwards to run,
with the other champions
all gazing up in the snow of hope,
a beauty she has imagined
only on the pages and in the tattling talks.
Weird thing fear is
unseen and wild
like the air of the hill.
She keeps exceeding one rock over another,
as stopping by the steep cliffs and wildflowers
seems no alternative
as nights become harder when she closes her eyes.
Days, weeks, despair and faith
they all pass by and by

and none at the moment.
And there she reaches to the nearest point,
the flag someone posted, old but fluttering
up to the heavens.
I wonder what the mountaineer saw
at the top of all, beside the peak
among all the champions,
the everlasting climb to the
the other mountains
or, the void of all thoughts further
and now what more to climb.